EXTINCT SPECIES

EXTINCT UNDERWATER LIFE

**First published in 2002 by
Grolier Educational
Sherman Turnpike
Danbury, Connecticut 06816
© Quartz Editions 2002**

Library of Congress Cataloging-in-Publication Data

Extinct species.

     p. cm.

  Contents: v. 1. Why extinction occurs - - v. 2. Prehistoric animal life - - v. 3. Fossil
hunting - - v. 4. Extinct mammals - - v. 5. Extinct birds - - v. 6 Extinct underwater life - -
v. 7. Extinct reptiles and amphibians - - v. 8. Extinct invertebrates and plants - - v. 9.
Hominids - - v. 10. Atlas of extinction.

  Summary: Examines extinct species, including prehistoric man, and discusses why
extinction happens, as well as how information is gathered on species that existed
before humans evolved.

ISBN 0-7172-5564-6 (set) - - ISBN 0-7172-5565-4 (v. 1) - - ISBN 0-7172-5566-2 (v. 2)
- - ISBN 0-7172-5567-0 (v. 3) - - ISBN 0-7172-5568-9 (v. 4) - - ISBN 0-7172-5569-7 (v.
5) - - ISBN 0-7172-5570-0 (v. 6) - - ISBN 0-7172-5571-9 (v. 7) - - ISBN 0-7172-5572-7
(v. 8) - - ISBN 0-7172-5573-5 (v. 9) - - ISBN 0-7172-5574-3 (v. 10)

  1. Extinction (Biology) - - Juvenile literature. 2. Extinct animals - - Juvenile literature.
[1. Extinction (Biology) 2. Extinct animals.] I. Grolier Educational.

  QH78 .E88 2002
  578.68 - - dc21   2001055702

**Produced by Quartz Editions
Premier House
112 Station Road
Edgware HA8 7BJ
UK**

EDITORIAL DIRECTOR: Tamara Green
CREATIVE DIRECTOR: Marilyn Franks
PRINCIPAL ILLUSTRATOR: Neil Lloyd
CONTRIBUTING ILLUSTRATORS: Tony Gibbons, Helen Jones
EDITORIAL CONTRIBUTOR: Graham Coleman

Reprographics by Mullis Morgan, London
Printed in Belgium by Proost

ACKNOWLEDGMENTS

The publishers wish to thank the following for supplying
photographic images for this volume.

Front & back cover t SPL/J.Baum & D.Angus

Page 1t SPL/J.Baum & D.Angus;
p3t SPL/J.Baum & D.Angus; p25tl NHPA/N.Wu;
p25br NHPA/L. & B.Pitkin; p29tl OSF/W.Kennedy;
p34tr NHM; p34bl NHPA/Agence Nature;
p36cl OSF/Daniel Cox; p41tc NHM;
p41br NHPA/D.Heuclin; p42tr OSF/W.Gray;
p43br OSF/K.Gowlett-Holmes.

Abbreviations: Natural History Museum (NHM); Natural
History Photographic Agency (NHPA); Oxford Scientific Films
(OSF); Science Photo Library (SPL); bottom (b); center (c);
left (l); right (r); top (t).

EXTINCT SPECIES

EXTINCT UNDERWATER LIFE

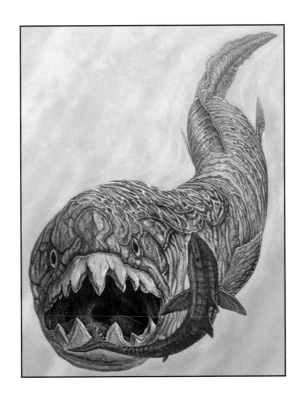

GROLIER EDUCATIONAL

SHERMAN TURNPIKE, DANBURY, CONNECTICUT 06816

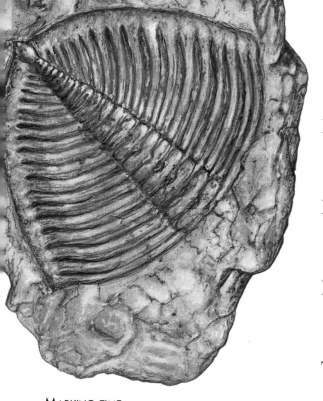

CONTENTS

MARKING TIME
Turn to pages 12-13 to discover what the fossilized creature shown *above*, a sort of geological timekeeper, has to tell us about the seas of the past.

MEET MESOSAURUS
There was no escape for any small fish that came up against this creature's brushlike jaws, as revealed on page 14.

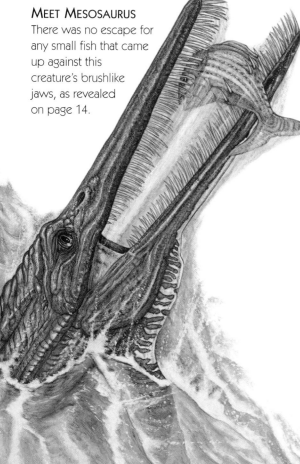

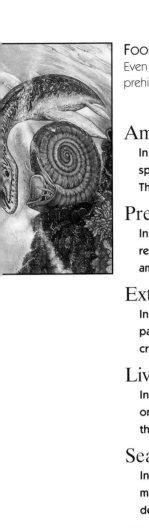

FOOD FOR THOUGHT
Even creatures with shells sometimes ended up as a prehistoric seafood dinner, as described on page 28.

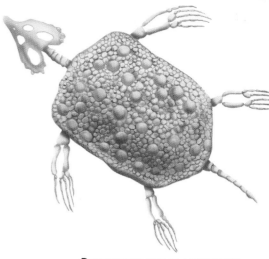

SEALED WITH A KISS
On pages 44-45 we examine some marine creatures now in severe decline and discuss how they might be saved from an untimely end.

PRESENTING THE PLACODONTS
Find out about their armored body structure, their movement over land and sea, and their staple diet by turning to pages 26-27.

NECK AND NECK
Some prehistoric sea creatures, like those *above*, had necks that seemed to go on forever. Discover which they were on pages 10-11.

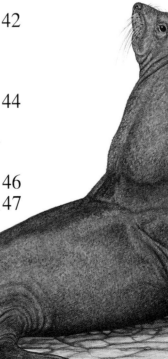

INTRODUCTION

Reports of sightings of enormous, unidentified, long-necked sea and lake monsters, as well as other peculiar marine animals, regularly appear in the press. Yet in most instances no one has produced proof as to whether they are prehistoric survivors or mere figments of the imagination. Certainly, some early sea creatures were most bizarre, and there is fossil evidence to prove this. Cretaceous ichthyosaurs, for instance, such as gigantic *Shonisaurus*, had massive, very menacing jaws. They also had powerful flippers and long, streamlined bodies ending in formidable tail flukes. These could be flicked back and forth, enabling the creatures to swim at sensational speeds so that they outpaced all other sea-dwellers.

A RIPPING TIME
Placodus, above, plentiful in the European seas of Triassic times, would open its mouth instinctively to rip away a meal of shellfish.

SHE SOLD SEASHELLS
Mary Anning, *above*, was a keen collector of fossils and came across many, including the remains of an ichthyosaur, near her home. She even opened a shop to sell fossils to the public.

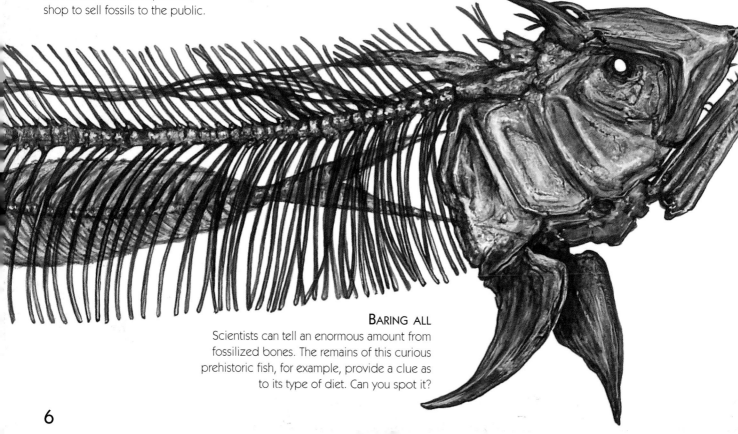

BARING ALL
Scientists can tell an enormous amount from fossilized bones. The remains of this curious prehistoric fish, for example, provide a clue as to its type of diet. Can you spot it?

One true survivor, however, which scientists know had identical ancestors 400 million years ago, from an era *predating* the dinosaurs, is the coelacanth. Once thought to be extinct, a specimen was rediscovered alive and well as the result of a chance sighting in the 20th century.

As you dive deep into this book, you will come face-to-face with some of the most interesting marine life ever to exist – just as 15-year-old Mary Anning did when she came across the first skeleton of a long-necked plesiosaur to be unearthed in the chalky cliffs near her home in Lyme Regis, England, back in 1814.

Discover, too, how another fascinating creature, Steller's sea cow, would regularly risk its life to save others of its species. Meet the marine monster that was the tyrant of the southern seas for over 130 million years. Marvel at the structure of ammonites and trilobites, and find out about the recent fate of the West Indian monk seal. There are some wonderful surprises in store!

A STRANGER RETURNS
No one was more astonished than the fishermen who hauled in this creature from South African waters. It turned out to be a coelacanth, previously thought extinct.

LONG-TAILED WHALES
Many early whales had a different shape from those we know today. The tail of *Basilosaurus*, for example, was very long and slim, as you can see here.

THE INSIDE STORY
Fossilized shells, like that of the ammonite *below*, were once home to live creatures.

ON ROCKY GROUND
This magnificent skeleton of an extinct sea creature was found by chance in the chalky cliffs of southern England.

PLIOSAURS

Dating from Early Jurassic times and surviving for 130 million years as a species, pliosaurs were mighty predators of the ocean. Paleontologists have found their remains on land masses as far apart as Australasia and Europe.

Strong flippers, a powerful tail, and slashing jaws – these were the principal features of the pliosaurs.

BULKY BEASTS

Pliosaurs were built for coping with far larger prey than such small fry, however, as their fossilized skeletons show, and so probably attacked at every opportunity. Even creatures the size of long-necked plesiosaurs, featured on pages 10-11, are likely to have ended up as their victims.

Smaller *pliosaurs*, however, such as one called *Peloneustes* (PEL-ON-OY-STEEZ), are likely to have cruised along in the waters, content to feed by biting chunks out of any more moderately sized quarry.

A SUITABLE NAME

The largest known pliosaur, *Kronosaurus* (KROH-NOH-SOR-US), was named for the mythological Greek god Kronos. Legend has it he devoured his children, so the name is apt for a greedy sea monster.

Their many sharp, closely packed teeth were slightly backward-curving, which made them all the more suitable for grasping at wriggling prey. But their mouths were so huge and cavernous that they probably only had to open them for a whole shoal of unsuspecting fish to swim in and be devoured as a snack in one great gulp.

VITAL STATISTICS
Kronosaurus, the largest of the pliosaurs discovered so far, was about 56 feet in length overall, but its head alone was 8 feet long. *Pliosaurus*, meanwhile, was far smaller – only about one-quarter that size; but even a 48-foot-long, dolphinlike ichthyosaur stood no chance against this creature.

Pliosaurs sometimes reached over 45 feet in length and had skulls that were longer than an adult human's arm and jaws with more biting power than one of today's killer whales.

ERROR OF JUDGMENT

Sometimes paleontologists are so eager to find the fossilized remains of larger and larger species that mistakes occur. In 1996, for example, on the basis of a single vertebra that had been found years earlier and stored in a small English museum, a paleontologist announced it came from a gigantic pliosaur, 40% larger than the record-holder, *Kronosaurus*. Experts then reexamined the specimen, which had come splattered with paint. It looked like a *pliosaur* neckbone, except it was far broader.

In the end everyone had to agree it was not a pliosaur vertebra after all but had been part of a giant sauropod dinosaur's skeleton.

But that is not all. There are doubts about other supposed pliosaur finds, too. Some experts even question the restored and mounted skeleton of a *Kronosaurus* in the collection held by the Harvard Museum of Comparative Zoology because so much plaster – and possibly s degree of imagination – was used for its reconstruction. A few paleontologists were so scathing about its identity that they even went so far as to dub it *Plastosaurus*!

More recently, possible pliosaur remains have also been found in Colombia, South America, and England, but await authentication.

BATTLE AT SEA
The illustration *below* shows a mighty pliosaur attacking a long- necked plesiosaur. The predatory pliosaur, with its huge jaws and sharp teeth, would surely have been the victor.

PLESIOSAURS

Sometimes described as ribbon reptiles because of their extraordinary necks, plesiosaurs swam the seas for over 100 million years during Jurassic and Cretaceous times. By the time they finally went extinct, some had evolved to reach lengths of over 40 feet.

Although completely at home in the sea, plesiosaurs could not breathe under water and so had to come up for air at regular intervals. But if their lungs had been much larger, scientists agree, they would have floated to the surface and would have been unable to dive for food or defend themselves.

Even though they were so big, plesiosaurs were often prime targets for hungry seagoing predators such as their close relatives, the pliosaurs, or the dolphinlike ichthyosaurs (<u>IK</u>-THEE-OH-SORS).

The longest plesiosaur found so far was discovered in Kansas, and another specimen has since been unearthed in Japan. *Elasmosaurus* (<u>EL</u>-AZ-MOH-<u>SOR</u>-US) had such a lengthy neck and tail that paleontologists described it as having been like a "snake threaded through the body of a turtle." In total it had 71 neck bones, but *you* only have seven! When it swam, a plesiosaur would have held its neck straight out in front of it. But when it rested, the neck could be coiled up.

Plesiosaur remains were first found by Mary Anning at Lyme Regis in southern England in 1814. Her father had instilled in her a fascination for paleontology, an unusual interest for a girl of that time. She loved piecing fossils together to reconstruct the original beast and, as you will find out later in this book, eventually opened a fossil shop of her own.

Its front flippers propelled a plesiosaur through the sea, while the back flippers were used for steering or for helping it come to a halt. Normally a graceful swimmer, at times a plesiosaur needed to be nifty in the water because it had no body weapons of any sort that could be used in the face of danger.

She certainly knew the value of fossils. Indeed, she eventually sold the plesiosaur remains she unearthed for about $150,000 in today's terms. The spot where she found this "treasure" remains a favorite fossil hunting area today, perhaps for this very reason.

10

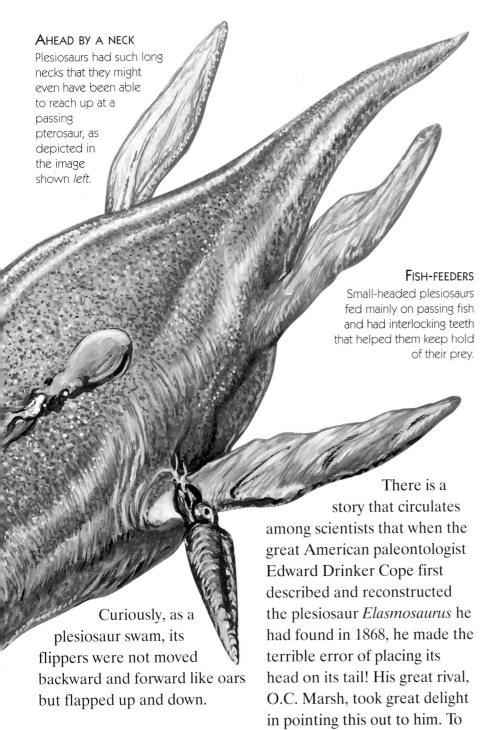

AHEAD BY A NECK

Plesiosaurs had such long necks that they might even have been able to reach up at a passing pterosaur, as depicted in the image shown *left*.

FISH-FEEDERS

Small-headed plesiosaurs fed mainly on passing fish and had interlocking teeth that helped them keep hold of their prey.

Curiously, as a plesiosaur swam, its flippers were not moved backward and forward like oars but flapped up and down.

SOLID EVIDENCE

These plesiosaur remains, embedded in rock, clearly show the bone structure of the ancient marine creature.

There is a story that circulates among scientists that when the great American paleontologist Edward Drinker Cope first described and reconstructed the plesiosaur *Elasmosaurus* he had found in 1868, he made the terrible error of placing its head on its tail! His great rival, O.C. Marsh, took great delight in pointing this out to him. To his dying day Cope felt very embarrassed by his error and resented Marsh's correction.

Fact file

- Plesiosaurs would have come onto land to lay the eggs from which their young hatched. The females probably laid several at a time, then covered them with sand or earth to provide sufficient warmth for incubation and so that they were safe from predators. After hatching, the young would have taken to the water almost immediately.

- The neck of a plesiosaur would have extended to over half its body length in some cases.

- A plesiosaur's head was tiny, but such a long, slim neck could not have supported a weightier skull.

- Amateur and professional fossil-hunters alike still find interesting remains near the site where Mary Anning found the first plesiosaur specimen.

SMOOTHLY DOES IT

A typical plesiosaur, the *Muraeonosaurus* (MU-REYE-OH-NOH-SOR-us) *above* swam gracefully in warm Cretaceous seas.

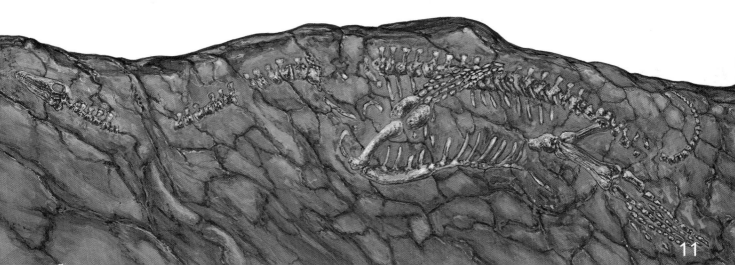

TRILOBITES

Amazingly hardy, thousands of different types of trilobites survived in the world's oceans for about 300 million years. Today these earliest arthropods – a group of creatures to which insects and spiders also belong – have much to reveal in their fossilized form about Earth's geological record.

Scientists can tell a lot about the original appearance of the trilobites from their remains. A dominant form of marine life until the end of the Permian period, they had well-armored bodies divided into three main sections, hence their name, which means "three-lobed."

All had head shields, a segmented thorax, and a tail; but they evolved into a whole variety of most fantastic shapes as they adapted to changing environments. Some had a spiky exterior that provided a degree of protection against enemies; but others would curl up into a ball together if threatened.

SAFETY IN NUMBERS
Some trilobites, such as the one *above*, were able to join forces and roll up into a ball together to protect themselves if danger threatened.

Some were the size of a lobster; others looked more like broad beans and would swarm together so that the sea became black with them. Some had projections that resembled horns; others had growths that looked like tridents. Most dwelt at the bottom of the oceans, where they scavenged or fed on detritus. But some may even have been predatory.

From whatever viewpoint you look at them – from the side, from the front, or from above – they are all a never-ending source of fascination.

EYES ON YOU
The large-eyed trilobite in the illustration *left* was found in the United States but had a worldwide distribution.

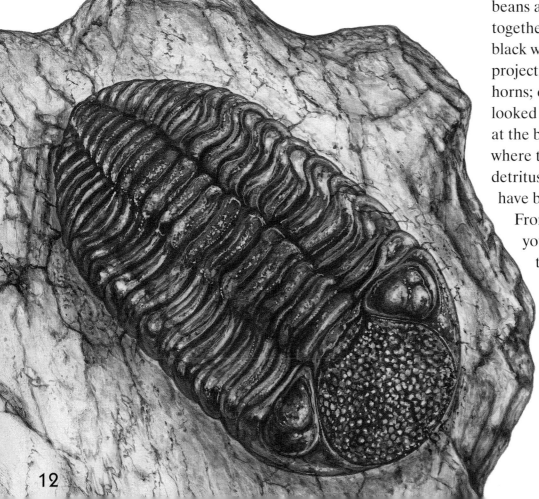

Each type also developed different organs of sight. There is evidence that some – *Neoasaphus* (<u>NEE</u>-OH-<u>SAF</u>-US), for instance – even had eyes at the end of protruding stalks. They could be retracted until the trilobites needed to inspect their surroundings for predators or perhaps prey. A number, however, had no vision at all.

Where eyes existed, they were made of a substance called clear calcite that provided lenses as tough as a clam's shell.

Specific types of trilobites would have lived in particular regions. Some of those unearthed in Canada, for example, are like a number found in Scotland, so that it seems likely the two countries were once linked, perhaps by a sort of land bridge.

One type of trilobite, meanwhile, known as *Calymene* (<u>KAL</u>-EE-MEEN), had an exceptionally vast geographic range and has been found in Europe and Australia, as well as North and South America.

Fact file

● On average trilobites were about 4 inches long, but some larger species grew to over 2 feet in length.

● Trilobites first appeared on Earth 545 million years ago in the Cambrian period.

● There were many thousands of species of trilobites, and they varied greatly in shape.

● Trilobites liked salty waters and thrived on the continental shelves of the world's oceans.

● Very early trilobites were soft, so there is little fossil evidence of them. But later species had hard shells that fossilized well. Trilobites also left tracks that over millions of years have formed trace fossils.

● Today's horseshoe crabs are like the trilobites of prehistoric times in many ways.

UNSIGHTED SPECIMEN
This fossilized trilobite was found in what is now the Czech Republic and measures just over two inches in length. There are no signs of eyes. Similar types of trilobites have been found in Australia, North and South America, and other parts of Europe.

PROLIFIC BREEDERS
Paleontologists also know that trilobites must have reproduced regularly and in huge numbers, but no one is certain how they mated since there is no evidence of sexual differences in the fossils found.

They may have been hermaphrodites of some kind; and a small swelling in the head-end of some types is thought possibly to have been a sort of pouch for carrying the young, much as marsupials do.

CRUCIAL EVIDENCE
The huge variety of trilobite fossils has also proved very useful to geologists who are studying separation of the world's land masses into continents.

Trilobites were most common during Carboniferous times, which lasted from 345 to 280 million years ago. But during the subsequent Permian period the fossil record shows that this arthropod vanished completely. No one is sure why, but the most likely explanation is that sea levels fell, draining continental shelves of the warm waters in which the trilobites had formerly thrived. Their favored habitat slowly shrank and then finally disappeared. Trilobites survived on Earth for 300 million years – a very long time when you consider that humans have only existed for about half of 1% of that!

MESOSAURUS

Only 16 inches in length at the most, but with long, snappy jaws, *Mesosaurus* (<u>MEEZ</u>-OH-<u>SOR</u>-US) lived back in Permian times and probably became extinct long before the dinosaurs had evolved. Although it lived in the water, it went ashore to lay its eggs.

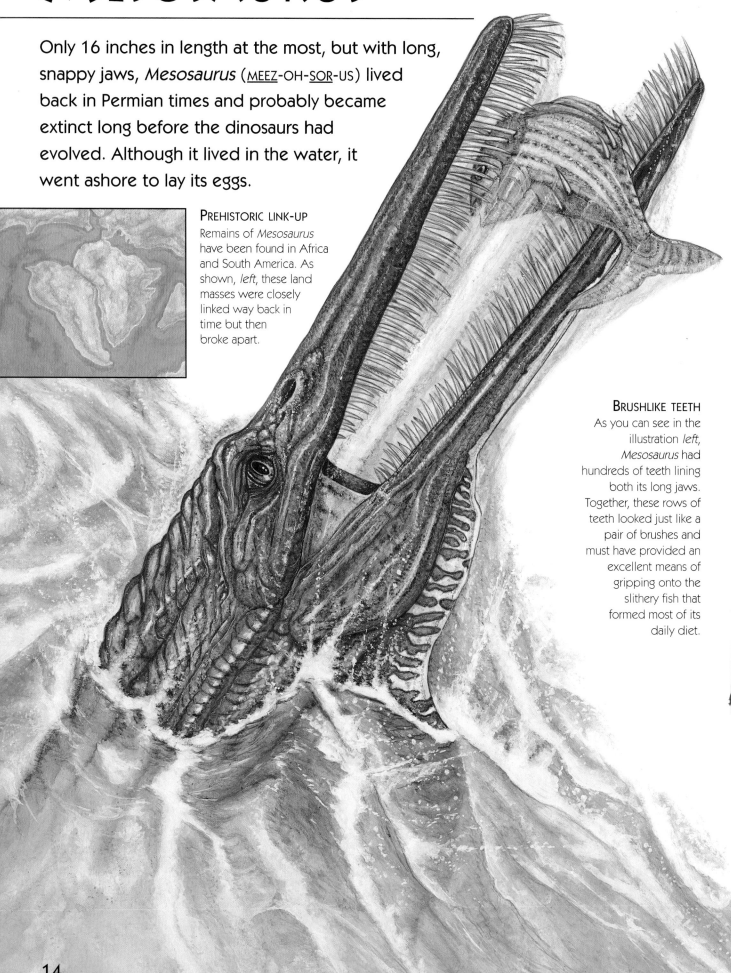

PREHISTORIC LINK-UP
Remains of *Mesosaurus* have been found in Africa and South America. As shown, *left*, these land masses were closely linked way back in time but then broke apart.

BRUSHLIKE TEETH
As you can see in the illustration *left*, *Mesosaurus* had hundreds of teeth lining both its long jaws. Together, these rows of teeth looked just like a pair of brushes and must have provided an excellent means of gripping onto the slithery fish that formed most of its daily diet.

Mesosaurs are classed as reptile synapsids, which means that in their skulls there were two openings – one above and one below a central area.

First unearthed in southern Africa in 1864, mesosaurs – the family to which *Mesosaurus* belongs – have also been found in eastern Brazil, South America, and Antarctica. These discoveries of creatures that lived 280 million years ago were of course wonderfully exciting. But that was not all. Their fossilized remains have also enabled scientists to confirm an important theory.

ON THE MOVE

If you look at a world map today, it is perhaps obvious that at one time all the landmasses might have fitted together, just like the pieces of a giant jigsaw, with sea all around them. But until a German geophysicist, Alfred Wegener, first suggested the continents might once have been joined together, no one had so far given the matter much thought.

The theory he put forward was that, long ago, Europe and Africa had drifted apart from North and South America. However, the public was skeptical about this since he could offer no explanation as to the cause. But we now know there is constant activity under the oceans, and that the continents float on great sheets of the Earth's crust called tectonic plates.

Mesosaurus 200 P·00

GUINÉ-BISSAU
correios 1989

POSTAL TRIBUTE
The postage stamp shown *left* was issued in 1989 by the African state of Guinea-Bissau and features a snarling *Mesosaurus*, remains of which have been found on the African continent.

Back in Permian times, all land was linked together in one huge continent known as Pangaea, meaning "all Earth." That was when mesosaurs were to be found.

Only in Triassic times did this supercontinent start to break up into two landmasses known as Laurasia and Gondwana. They later broke up further until the world took on the shape it has today.

The fact that mesosaurs have been found as far apart as South America and Africa, when they could not possibly have swum such a distance, lends further credence to the theory that these two continents were once part of the same landmass.

In any event, they would not have taken to the oceans. As we know from the rocks in which they have been discovered, they enjoyed a different environment.

Fact file

- *Mesosaurus* had an exceptionally long skull.
- The teeth of the mesosaur family were so thin and numerous that they were more like the spiky tufts of a brush than true teeth.
- The weight of *Mesosaurus* is unknown, but it is unlikely to have been more than a few pounds since they were so small. Being lightweight no doubt helped them move swiftly through the water both to catch their prey and to escape from predators themselves.
- Mesosaurs were already extinct well before dinosaurs had started to evolve.
- *Mesosaurus* may have had webbed feet. That would have helped if they came onto land to lay their eggs.

Their natural habitat was to be found in freshwater lakes. But here, too, they were at risk of being chased by far larger marine predators.

SMALL AND SWIFT
Mesosaurus had a long tail, as this fossil clearly shows, which would have helped it swim well. Its remains also suggest that it had webbed feet.

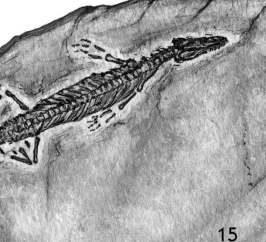

MORE MARINE REPTILES

In prehistoric times, over hundreds of millions of years a whole variety of sea creatures appeared on this planet only, for many reasons, to become extinct. A large number were marine reptiles, which came in many different shapes and sizes.

If the waters of Cretaceous times were sometimes stained with blood, it may have been the result of a battle between two mosasaurs, for these 30-foot-long creatures were very territorial.

ON LAND AND SEA

Triassic *Nothosaurus* (NOH-THOH-SOR-US), *below*, spent a lot of time in the sea but could also come onto land. Its strong but supple neck would have helped it fish from a rocky outcrop or cliff.

They grew to be 30 feet in length and had rows of backward-pointing teeth that were suited to tearing at flesh. Although they were reptiles, they had lost the ability to come onto land, which meant the females could not leave the water to lay their eggs. Instead, they kept their eggs inside their bodies and then, when the eggs hatched, they delivered live young, just like some snakes.

Tylosaurus (TEYE-LOH-SOR-US), a species of mosasaur, has been found in Kansas and in New Zealand; another, *Hainosaurus* (HAY-NOH-SOR-US), was discovered in Belgium.

CRYPTIC FEATURE

The most distinctive attribute of 10-foot-long *Cryptocleidus* (KRIPT-OH-KLEYE-DUS), whose remains have been found in England, was its neck. It was snakelike and not nearly as long as the necks of most other plesiosaurs.

IN JURASSIC WATERS

Jurassic European seas were home to *Temnodontosaurus* (<u>TEM</u>-NOH-<u>DONT</u>-OH-<u>SOR</u>-US), an enormous, long-snouted and sharp-toothed creature that grew to 30 feet in length. Its strong flippers probably helped it swim after prey at great speed.

DINOSAUR DILEMMA

Over the last 100 years, there has been great debate over whether dinosaurs could swim, and how often they took to the water. Were some in fact *marine* reptiles?

Lots of fossilized dinosaur footprints have been found in rocks that are also imprinted with ripples, which indicates they were not afraid to get their feet wet. But did they merely paddle, or were they true swimmers, like plesiosaurs?

Experts studying tracks left by giant sauropods in a part of Texas that was a coastal region in Jurassic times think they often crossed narrow, shallow stretches of water in search of food. They may also have gone into lakes to escape the clutches of a predator or to suck up underwater foliage. However, experts now agree that dinosaurs could not swim as such and would never have crossed the wide oceans.

MAKING MEAT OF DINOSAURS

A crocodilian with a huge mouth, *Phobosuchus* (<u>FOH</u>-BOH-<u>SOOK</u>-US) grew to as long as 50 feet, and many species of dinosaur would have found it a fearsome predator.

PREHISTORIC FISH

Fish were the first of our planet's vertebrate (backboned) animals, and many that look strange to us today took a hold in the seas, rivers, and lakes as far back as Devonian times – that is, about 400 million years ago.

SUIT OF ARMOR

Dating from 395 to 345 million years ago, the flat fish, a *Gemuendina* (JEM-OO-END-EE-NAH), *below*, was armored with bony plates and looked much like a present-day skate, with its extended fins. and very wide head.

From the fossil record we can tell that the fish of Devonian times were numerous and varied. Some were also unusual in shape and had heavily armored bodies instead of the soft scales that most fish have today.

Paleontologists have found four types of early fish. The chondrichthians (KON-DRIK-THEE-ANS) includesharks, which you can read about on pages 40-41.

SUCKING UP

The ostracoderms (OST-RAK-OH-DERMS) were far smaller fish, only 20 inches in length, and without jaws of any kind. All they had for mouths were thin slits. Through them they could suck up water and plankton. Some had flattened head shields and eyes on top of their heads. Others had tough scales, fed on mud, and may be related to modern lampreys, which look like eels.

The osteichthians (OST-EYEK-THEE-ANS), or bony fish, of prehistoric times comprised two types – the lobe-finned fishes (so-called because their fins rose from scale-covered lobes or stocky appendages of muscle) and the ray-fins, of which thousands of different species exist today. Some early bony fish may even have been able to survive out of the water.

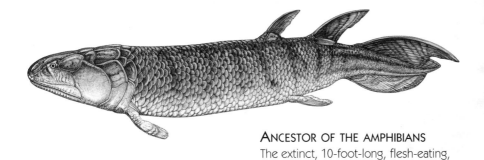

This probably occurred because they had no alternative in times of drought, when they would have struggled hard to reach another body of water. And because paleontologists have noticed the fins of a bony fish known as *Eusthenopteron* (<u>YOO</u>-STEN-<u>OPT</u>-ER-ON) are in exactly the same position as the legs of primitive amphibians, it is thought to have evolved into these creatures over millions of years.

BOTTOM-DWELLERS

But the most fearsome of all fish of Devonian times were undoubtedly the placoderms (the name means "plated skin"). They were fierce predators, lurking and feeding at the bottom of the sea. Armored heads and huge jaws were their principal features. Their overall body size was gigantic, too. An example is *Dunkleosteus* (<u>DUNK</u>-LEE-<u>OST</u>-EE-US), truly a marine marvel, which you will find illustrated on page 40. Some placoderms are thought to have moved by dragging themselves along in the mud; others swam or may have used their spiked fins to "walk" as if on stilts.

ANCESTOR OF THE AMPHIBIANS
The extinct, 10-foot-long, flesh-eating, lobe-finned fish *above*, *Eusthenopteron*, was from Devonian times and a possible ancestor of the first amphibians.

FEEDING HABITS

In general, the development of jaws led to far greater feeding possibilities for such early fish. They could now munch on creatures like the giant crustaceans of Devonian times, some of which were an astounding 10 feet in length.

The placoderms' bony plates covered not only their heads but also the front part of their bodies, giving them valuable protection against attack. Almost certainly, the enormous water scorpions of the time would have tried to resist. So even creatures as sizable and tough as the placoderms had to be on their guard.

Now turn the page to find out about other extinct fish. As you will also discover, more and more marine species are becoming endangered with every passing year.

MORE LOST FISH

Other types of fish began to evolve during Late Jurassic and Cretaceous times, when dinosaurs ruled. Among them were the first teleosts, of which there are around 20,000 species today. But in the 21st century, too, numerous fish continue to disappear from our waters.

The very first bony fish opened their mouths in a very simple way, just as you do. However, the teleosts (TEL-EE-OSTS) – of which such fish as carp, salmon, cod, herrings, eel, and tuna are a few present-day examples – could and still can project their jaws forward, helping them suck in their prey and almost literally vacuum up food from the ocean bed.

Early teleosts reached considerable proportions, and fossilized remains have been found extending to 17 feet.

THE HUMAN FACTOR

According to an old saying, there are plenty of fish in the sea. But marine biologists report many are fast disappearing from our oceans, rivers, and lakes, due principally to human interference.

No shortnose sucker fish, for example, have been seen in Upper Klamath Lake, Oregon, since around 1960. That is almost certainly due to the building of a dam where they formerly spawned.

The North American deepwater cisco was also once abundant in Lakes Michigan and Huron, but it has not been seen for over 40 years. Over-fishing has been blamed, although the lampreys introduced to these waters may have become so dominant that the cisco simply could not compete. In much the same way a flat-headed fish, once found only in Lake Titicaca, on the border of Peru and Brazil, also became extinct when a species of predatory trout was introduced to the lake.

Changes to the natural environment of a species can have devastating effects, too; and that is why ecologists think the very last fat-tailed dace, once so common in California, was caught in 1945. Serious deformities in some fish have also recently become apparent due to pollutant minerals, such as mercury, carelessly emptied into our seas.

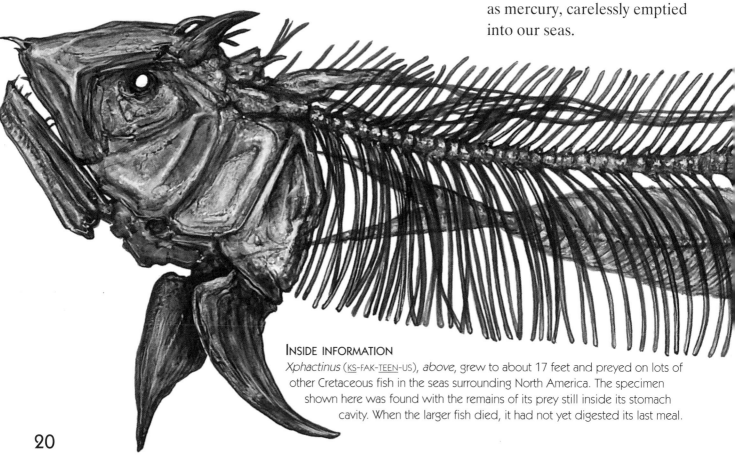

INSIDE INFORMATION
Xphactinus (KS-FAK-TEEN-US), *above*, grew to about 17 feet and preyed on lots of other Cretaceous fish in the seas surrounding North America. The specimen shown here was found with the remains of its prey still inside its stomach cavity. When the larger fish died, it had not yet digested its last meal.

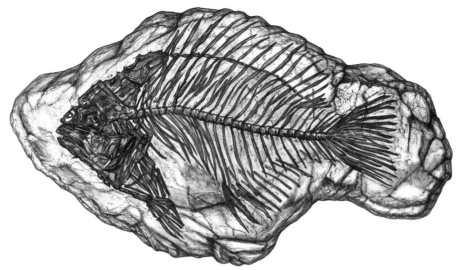

DYING FOR DOLLARS

The aquarium trade has also frequently been blamed for the gradual decline in some rare tropical breeds. Many billions of dollars are spent worldwide each year by those who keep fish, but too few seem to be aware of the depletion effect. In some parts of the world tropical fish are also taken in very cruel ways. A highly toxic cyanide solution, for instance, is sometimes squirted at them, causing the fish to become drowsy. They are then collected by a suction process.

MAKING AN IMPRESSION
The superbly preserved fossil *above* is of a teleost from North America. It dates from Eocene times and is characterized by a perfectly symmetrical tail.

According to one estimate, 80% of all tropical fish taken in this way die within a short time. Others perish due to overcrowding while being transported. Related stress and disease will also take their toll. What is more, some species of fish are entirely unsuited to life in an aquarium.

Fact file

● In prehistoric times fish are most likely to have disappeared altogether only when mass extinctions occurred. In more modern times, however, humans have been to blame.

● Pollution of rivers, lakes, and seas is increasingly leading to the demise of lots of different species of fish.

● When new species of fish have been introduced to a river or lake, they have sometimes proved predatory or very greedy that they prevented those fish already there from finding sufficient food, so that they died out.

● Now more than ever, commercial fishing is an enterprise that needs to be very carefully managed to avoid depletion of stock.

We can do nothing to bring back the wonderful extinct fish of prehistoric times, but every effort needs to be made to ensure none of those endangered today vanishes forever.

ICHTHYOSAURS

Looking remarkably similar to today's dolphins and with a name meaning "fish lizards," this group of marine reptiles had no neck, four limbs that resembled paddles, and a fishlike tail. They were extremely well suited to life in the ocean; but fossilized remains found in Nevada show that at least on one occasion a whole community of them beached themselves, just as whales sometimes do today.

Most of these aquatic predators were around 13-16 feet in length and could probably swim at a considerable rate. They first arose in the Early Triassic, and some types populated the seas until well into the Cretaceous. One of them was *Shonisaurus* (SHOH-NEE-SOR-US), a giant among ichthyosaurs, extending to all of 50 feet. Its huge jaws must have been highly menacing.

EVIDENCE OF DISASTER
An artist's impression, *right*, shows how a whole group of *Shonisaurus*, though usually in the ocean, must had beached themselves for some mysterious reason, to judge from the many remains found in one Nevada location.

Creatures as large as plesiosaurs, as well as early sharks, were fair game for ichthyosaurs. Otherwise, when no such substantial meals presented themselves, they would have fed on huge quantities of ammonites and belemnites. Indeed, as many as 1,600 such undigested mollusks were found in the stomach cavity of a single specimen.

Fossil-finder

During the 19th century Mary Anning, shown *left* in her fossil shop at Lyme Regis, southern England, searched every day by the cliffs near her home for fossil remains; and although she had no formal training, she was skilled at reconstructing the skeletons of prehistoric creatures. Among her finds were ichthyosaur and pterosaur remains and the plesiosaur fossil you can see on page 11.

What a snout!

Found in Europe, the sea creature *Eurhinosaurus* (<u>YOOR</u>-EEN-OH-<u>SOR</u>-US), shown here, was dolphin-shaped, like all ichthyosaurs, but had the most extraordinarily long nose

Mixed features

Mixosaurus, the ichthyosaur shown *above*, had small flippers that acted as paddles, a fishlike tail, and no distinct neck. It has been unearthed in Europe and may have grown to reach 40 feet in length. Like all ichthyosaurs, it gave birth to live young.

We now know, however, that they were in fact embryo ichthyosaurs. Unable to lay eggs on land, ichthyosaurs were ovoviviparous and would keep their eggs' inside them until they could give birth to live young, which were born head-first, like whales.

Inside one set of remains paleontologists found 11 tiny embryos, leading them to the conclusion that multiple births must have been common.

Some fossilized remains from quarries near Stuttgart in Germany are so well preserved that miniature skeletons of what must have been ichthyosaur prey have been found inside them.

At first some scientists thought this was evidence of cannibalism and that they sometimes ate their young.

For some unknown reason ichthyosaurs died out about 30 million years before the dinosaurs. During their time on the planet, however, they must have been among the strongest of swimmers, swinging their bodies and tail fins from side to side as they moved in the water, and using their front flippers for steering.

Fact file

- *Shonisaurus* was 50 feet long and the largest ichthyosaur found so far. Fossilized remains show that, unlike other ichthyosaurs, it only had teeth at the front of its mouth.

- Ichthyosaurs have been described as the "acrobats of the sea." That is because paleontolgists think their streamlined bodies made them excellent divers, just as dolphins are today.

- Ichthyosaurs were probably able to swim at speeds of up to 30 miles per hour with the help of their massive tail flukes, which acted as accelerators.

- Finally, ichthyosaurs may have become extinct because they failed to adapt to the tremendous environmental changes that eventually engulfed the planet.

Paleontologists have used clues provided by fossilized ichthyosaur remains to assess their behavior. From the ring of strengthening bone around their eyes, for example, we can tell that these marine predators would have been capable of diving to considerable depths in pursuit of their prey.

In 1957, in Nevada an area was officially designated Ichthyosaur State Park to protect and display North America's most ichthyosaur-rich fossil site. In all, it covers over 1,000 acres. More recently, the ichthyosaur has also been declared the Nevada state fossil.

ARCHELONS

Giant sea turtles, archelons (<u>ARK</u>-EL-ONS) lived in Late Cretaceous times and grew to weigh as much as one ton. They probably died out 65 million years ago, along with the dinosaurs and other large marine reptiles. But can we be sure about this?

Turtles first arose in Late Triassic times and remained mainly on land for many millions of years.

But by the Late Cretaceous, about 80 million years ago, some had begun to inhabit the seas and turned into fish-eaters. Archelons are thought to have been the largest of them all and were certainly far bigger than any of the turtles we know today.

As fossilized remains found in North America clearly show, their carapaces (shells) were extremely lightweight and so did not hinder movement. But they were also tough enough to withstand attack by all but the most scything teeth. Scientists are unsure, however, whether this turtle had already developed the ability to withdraw its head, tail, or legs into its shell to protect these soft bodyparts in the face of danger. If so, it would definitely have stood far more chance of survival when confronted by predators.

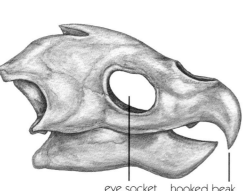

eye socket   hooked beak

HEADLINE NEWS
The skull of an archelon, *above*, shows a hooked beak that may have been used to crack open shellfish.

GREAT ESCAPE
Archelons were probably often chased along the beach by enormous carnivorous dinosaurs, eager to make a meal of them. But provided they reached the sea in time, they would be safe since dinosaurs were unable to swim.

PROTECTING THE NEXT GENERATION
Just as turtles do today, archelons would bury their eggs in the sand to keep them warm during incubation. All the while, they would also be safe from predators.

Earlier turtles, such as *Triassochelys* (TREYE-AS-OK-EEL-IS), which lived in Triassic times, definitely could not withdraw their heads, tails, and limbs. Its neck and tail, however, were partly protected by small spikes, as remains from central Europe, now on display at natural history museums in Berlin, Germany, and London, England, clearly show.

ENEMY ACTION

Each year, just like the sea turtles of today, archelons probably returned to the same shorelines, gathering in their thousands to lay their eggs. But it would have been a risky and exhausting business. It must have taken a considerable time for them to heave their hefty bodies along the beach, so that they were constantly vulnerable to attack. Indeed, a sizable theropod could only too easily have turned turtles onto their backs so that they became completely helpless.

The enemy could then feast on archelon belly meat while the turtles were still alive, leaving behind their upturned shells.

Archelon eggs would also have made a tasty meal for any passing predator. However, the females buried them in the sand, exactly as turtles do today, so the next generation could hatch safely. Then it would be a matter of luck as to whether the newborn turtles got to the ocean in time.

The largest recognized turtle today is the leathery species, which may grow to 9 feet in length. But occasional reports come to light of the sighting of even larger turtles. In the 19th century, for example, one turned up off Newfoundland and was at first mistaken for a capsized boat; and in 1956, while near Nova Scotia, the crew of a cargo steamer claimed they had spotted a live giant turtle, just like an archelon, that was 45 feet long with a white carapace.

Could it be that in some parts of the world archelons have somehow survived and still lurk in our oceans?

TAKING A DIVE
The swimming action of this marine green turtle, seen in waters off the island of Borneo, Malaysia, is probably very similar to that of the ancient turtle archelon.

PLACODONTS

With a name meaning "flat teeth," this group of creatures was among the first reptiles on our planet to move into the water more than 215 million years ago. They seem to have been plentiful in the seas around what is now Europe, and particularly in the region of Italy.

Not entirely aquatic and in some ways more suited to getting around on land than in water, placodonts nevertheless probably spent a good part of their day in the warm shallows during Triassic times, when they first appeared. Here, as remains found in their stomach area and mouth structure show, they feasted on large quantities of shellfish.

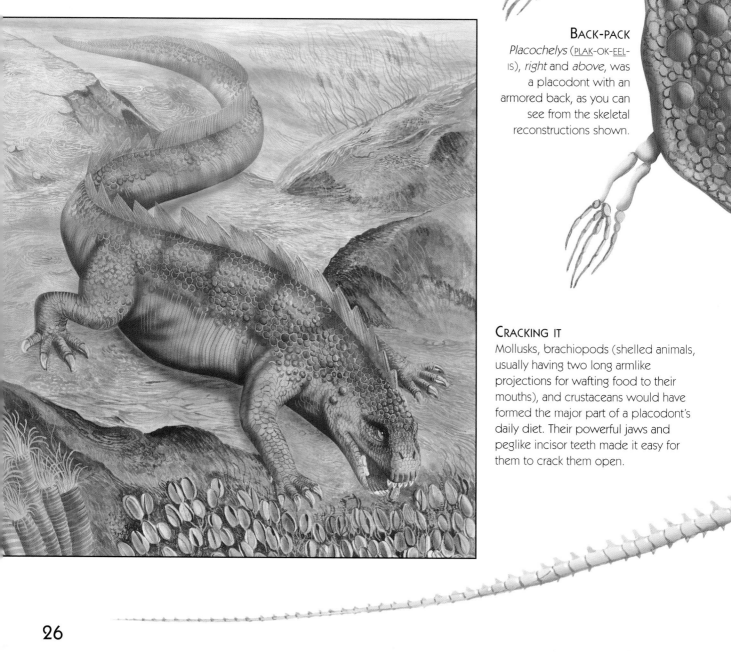

BACK-PACK

Placochelys (<u>PLAK</u>-OK-<u>EEL</u>-IS), *right* and *above*, was a placodont with an armored back, as you can see from the skeletal reconstructions shown.

CRACKING IT

Mollusks, brachiopods (shelled animals, usually having two long armlike projections for wafting food to their mouths), and crustaceans would have formed the major part of a placodont's daily diet. Their powerful jaws and peglike incisor teeth made it easy for them to crack them open.

Mollusks were torn from the seabed with their powerfully muscled, shovel-shaped jaws and the six sharp, peglike front teeth (incisors) that made them a very special sort of Triassic reptile.

Then their 14 blunt, flat, crushing back teeth, which were covered with thick enamel, would be used for grinding up the meal.

The resulting mush, a mixture of cephalopods, such as belemnites that closely resembled today's squid, and clams would then have been easy to digest.

The placodont known as *Placodus* may even have had a functioning third eye that would have helped it spot a predator more readily. Its scaly skin, meanwhile, provided a degree of protection against greedy predators.

Other placodonts, however, such as *Placochelys* and *Henodus*, dug up from Triassic layers near the town of Tübingen in Germany, had far tougher body armor that resembled a turtle's shell, even though they are not related to the turtle family.

These two placodonts may also have had no teeth near the front of their jaws but probably a horny beak instead.

Mysteriously, there is no evidence of the placodonts surviving beyond the Late Triassic, and so they probably died out around 200 million years ago. At around this time there appears to have been a mass extinction.

Fact file

● Placodonts are thought usually to have walked across the sea floor in search of meals of crustacea but they also took to the land.

● They would have used not only their mouths but also their claws to take shellfish from rocky outcrops in the oceans.

● Placodont jaws were operated by very powerful muscles.

● Since they were so slow-moving, placodonts were probably vulnerable to attack; but their tough body armor would have provided some protection from both land and sea predators of the time.

● Placodonts had short but strong legs that splayed outward.

● Some placodonts had far longer tails than others.

One theory put forward by paleontologists suggests it may have been due to the increasing prevalence of dinosaurs during this period; another, that a marked shift from regular, heavy rainfall to a much drier type of climate may have been the cause.

UNDERNEATH IT ALL
As you can see from this reconstruction of the skeleton of the placodont known as *Placodus*, beneath its armor plating it had a body structure similar to that of other reptiles.

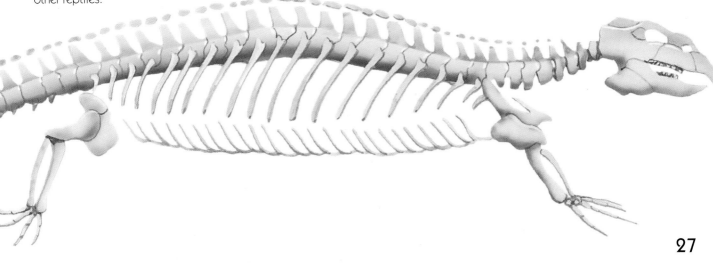

AMMONITES

These fascinating marine creatures lived within coiled shells during Jurassic and Cretaceous times. Billions of their fossils now remain and are surprisingly inexpensive to buy, considering their great age. Sometimes they are polished and made into jewelry.

Some ammonites were tiny and only about half an inch across at the most. Others were enormous in comparison, the size of your arm in diameter or even larger.

They have been found almost all over the world, including the United States, Europe, the Himalayas, as far north as Greenland, Africa, Japan, Russia, and New Zealand.

IN GOOD SHAPE

Their shells always featured a few spiraling coils that looked like rams' horns and give the ammonites their distinctive shape. (This is in fact also how the ammonites got their name, which was borrowed from the great Egyptian deity Amun, who was sometimes depicted with a ram's head.)

Later, ammonite fossils were sometimes called snakestones due to a mistaken belief that their coiled form showed they had originally been serpents.

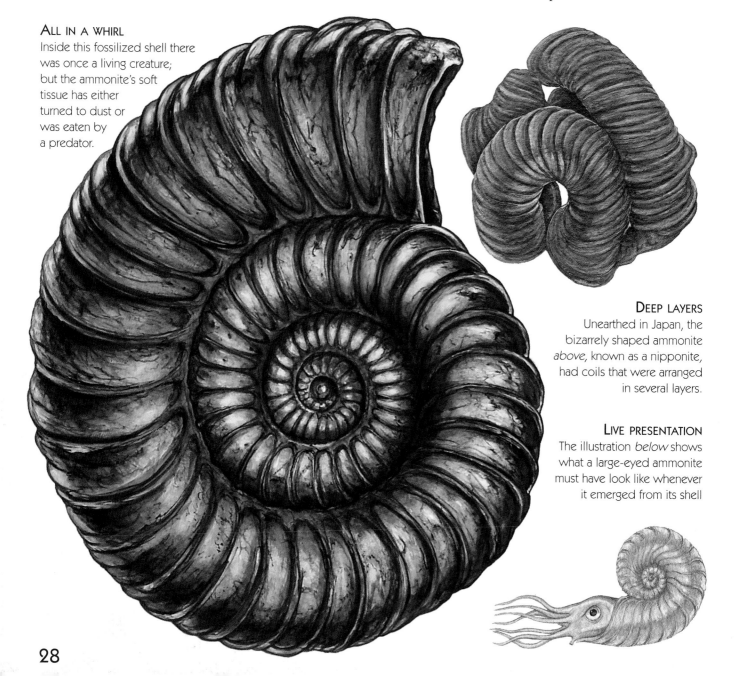

ALL IN A WHIRL
Inside this fossilized shell there was once a living creature; but the ammonite's soft tissue has either turned to dust or was eaten by a predator.

DEEP LAYERS
Unearthed in Japan, the bizarrely shaped ammonite *above*, known as a nipponite, had coils that were arranged in several layers.

LIVE PRESENTATION
The illustration *below* shows what a large-eyed ammonite must have look like whenever it emerged from its shell

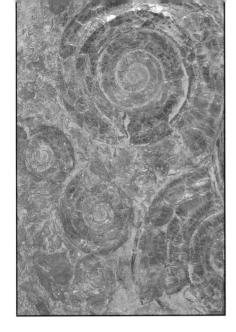

WHORLS WITHIN WHORLS
The photograph *left* shows fossilized ammonites still embedded in their original rock. There were a great many different types, but all had a coiled structure of some kind.

Fact file

● Some ammonite fossils have been found with puncture marks, which suggests that other sea creatures had tried to get at the live creature inside the shell.

● Ammonite fossils were once thought to provide a cure for both baldness and infertility if worn around the neck as lucky charms, but there is no proof that this odd remedy ever worked for anyone.

● Ammonites ranged from smaller than your little fingernail to 3 feet in diameter.

● Scientists do not know for sure what color ammonite shells originally were, but think they may well have varied. Whatever their coloring, it is likely to have provided them with a degree of camouflage.

Sometimes ammonite shells would also feature spines and other small projections that would give the creature inside them added protection. Otherwise a whole assortment of predators might have found it only too easy to crack open the shell and gobble up the soft body within. Some ammonite fossils even have clear puncture marks on the shell, indicating they had been attacked. Ammonites themselves, meanwhile, fed on the minute plankton and marine plants of prehistoric times.

INSIDE STORY
But what did the fleshy creatures inside these shells look like? They had large eyes and many tentacles that, if danger threatened, could be withdrawn into the outer shell.

The interior of the shell was divided into three chambers separated by walls known as septa. The animal itself lived in the very last chamber, while the others were filled with a sort of liquid gas. Through careful regulation of the contents of these two chambers, the ammonite could control its movement in the sea.

But ammonites also had another remarkable means of propulsion. If they wanted to move speedily, they could squirt out a jet of water that would then send them shooting backward rather than forward, with luck to a safer spot.

HIDE-AND-SEEK
All sorts of prehistoric sea creatures would have preyed on the ammonites, as shown *right*. But they would withdraw into their tough, coiled shells as soon as they sensed an approach, so that only the most tenacious predators would get through to their fleshy parts.

PREHISTORIC SURVIVORS?

Every now and then there are reported sightings of huge lake and sea monsters in places as far apart as Loch Lomond in Scotland, Canada, and Africa. Has it always been a case of mistaken identity, or could they be throwbacks to creatures thought long extinct?

One of the arguments often put forward for the continued existence of creatures resembling the plesiosaurs of prehistoric times is that there are other creatures alive today – turtles, dragonflies, and crocodiles, to cite only a few – whose ancestors somehow managed to survive the extinction of the dinosaurs 65 million years ago.

In 1974, for example, a young woman swimming in the waters of Lake Okanagan, British Columbia, Canada, claimed to have been startled as she felt herself buffeted by a long, muscular shape which pushed past. Then, suddenly, she saw in front of her, rising above the surface of the calm waters, several fleshy coils.

Each undulating coil was several feet long and about 3 feet across, and the skin was smooth and hairless. As this eyewitness later told a society of cryptozoologists (scientists who study evidence for the existence of strange creatures): *"The tail was forked and horizontal, like a whale's .... As the hump submerged, the tail came to the surface until its tip poked about a foot above the water .... About 4 or 5 minutes passed from the time it bumped into me until the time it swam from view".*

If the swimmer's story is to be believed, she had possibly met with a sea-dweller known locally for hundreds of years by the curious name of Ogopogo.

Other creatures of similar appearance have been sighted in lakes all over the world, among them Lake Van in Turkey and Lake Ikeda in Japan. Indeed, to this day Japanese mothers do not allow their children to play near the lake, not only because they might fall in and drown but because they might meet the creature they call Issie.

OH, IT'S OGOPOGO!

The drawing shown here has been based on a description given by an eyewitness who claims to have seen the creature known as Ogopogo in a Canadian lake. Its resemblance to a plesiosaur is remarkable; but whether such prehistoric survivors actually exist or are all in the imagination has never been proven.

In 1981, north of San Francisco, several observers said they saw in the water a creature with humps lift its head to look around. It then moved out to the ocean.

There have been sightings, too, at Lake Champlain on the Canadian/United States border, and at Lake Khaiyr in eastern Siberia. In almost every instance the description given by seemingly entirely reliable eyewitnesses was similar. These marine creatures were said to be gray-blue in color, with a bulky body, a long neck, and a very small head.

In other parts of the world, however, these "modern plesiosaurs" have been described as having strange additional features, such as whiskers, horns, or other projections.

So could it all be put down to tricks of the light on water, mirages, hallucinations, or even wishful thinking? Or is the exciting rediscovery of the coelacanth, which you can read about on pages 34-35, an indication there may indeed exist lots of aquatic creatures throughout the world that somehow managed to carry on breeding in hiding, generation after generation, while thought to be long extinct?

FROM DOWN-UNDER?

Toward the end of the 19th century a teacher reported what she described as a placodermlike "monster turtle fish," near Australia's Great Barrier Reef. Strangely, several local people also claimed previously to have seen a similar creature, which they called by the Aboriginal name of Moha-moha.

Adding weight to such stories, as recently as 1986, a traveler to the Great Barrier Reef also said he had spotted what again looked exactly like a placoderm from Devonian times, as illustrated on page 40 of this book. He reckoned it was 70 feet in length. No placoderm fossils discovered so far show them to have been as large as that, however; so his estimate may well have been a gross exaggeration. As for the creature itself, since the supposed giant fish was not caught and, as far as we know, has not been since, we will probably never known whether it was all in the mind or a genuine sighting.

In any event, if placoderms are indeed still swimming in this region, surely many of the large numbers of divers who visit the Great Barrier Reef would have spotted them, too.

But perhaps if they do exist, they have become wary of humans. Then again, if they had indeed survived to this day, would we not have found examples of their fossils in post-Devonian rocks?

There is, of course, another possibility – that these creatures may not be throw-backs after all but entirely new species yet to be identified. It is an intriguing thought.

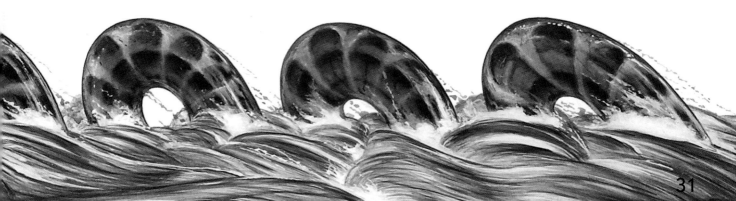

EXTINCT WHALES

Today there are more than 80 different species of whales, and the most extraordinary thing they have in common is the ancestor they share. It was a land animal that only started to take to the water 50 million years ago, long before we had evolved.

Modern whales are so well adapted to ocean life – swimming at a tremendous rate, diving to great depths, and subsisting on seafood – that it is hard to accept they evolved from a terrestrial ancestor.

It had a long snout, bulky body, four limbs, and probably a lengthy tail. In many ways it must have looked very piglike. While at home in the shallows, it was not yet ready, however, to take to deeper waters.

Whales are in fact an excellent example of the whole process of evolution; and by 40 million years ago, in Late Eocene times, these mammalians had probably become much more like the cetaceans (members of the whale family) we now know. They may even have started to reproduce in an entirely marine environment.

CHANGING OVER TIME
A landlubber, *Pakicetus, right,* from Eocene times, has been described as a whale-in-progress.

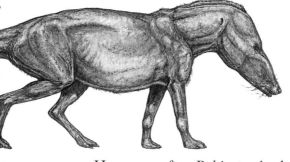

This early relative was *Pakicetus* (PAK-EE-SEET-US); and as you might guess from its name, remains were first discovered in Pakistan. It lived mostly on land, but ventured into water to cool down or chase prey. Even though only a few bones have been found so far, they have proved sufficient for paleontologists to draw conclusions about its appearance.

However, after *Pakicetus* had died out 50 million years ago, one of its relatives became sea-going. Indeed, some of its remains were also unearthed in Pakistan in 1994. Known by the scientific name *Ambulocetus* (AMB-YOO-LOH-SEET-US) which means "walking, swimming whale," it still probably came onto land for much of the time and would have mated and given birth out of the water.

TAIL FIRST
Once whales had begun to mate in the water, their young would have begun to be born tail first, just as they come into the world today. The head only appears at the very last moment, and the baby then severs the cord itself before swimming to the surface so that it can take its first breath. (If sea mammals were born head first, as humans and other land-based mammals usually are, they would probably drown.)

Among the first true whales were *Dorudon* (DOR-OO-DON), which resembled a porpoise, and its relative *Basilosaurus* (BAS-IL-OH-SOR-US), which had a longer head in proportion to its body than modern whales and irregular, triangular teeth.

Later, whales evolved into two main groups. One of them includes the baleen whales which still have no true teeth.

Instead, baleens of the past and those of today, including the bowheads and most of the larger whales, have comblike projections hanging from the top of their mouths. Through them food is strained from seawater intake. Among the toothed whales of both yesterday and today, meanwhile, are most of the smaller species.

A curious whalelike creature is even mentioned in the Bible.

Among the many mysteries of the Old Testament is the reference to a creature of the sea, known as the leviathan. According to the account in the book of *Isaiah*, it was enormous, toothed, and with a stocky neck and smoking nostrils. Some authorities claim the creature was a crocodile. However, others say the smoke described might possibly have been produced by an extinct whale's blowholes.

DRAMATIC DECLINE

Sadly, several species of whales are now severely endangered, among them the sperm whale, the gray whale, the humpback whale, the fin whale, and the 85-foot-long blue whale, one of the biggest creatures ever to have existed and certainly the largest mammal of the 21st century. Only through a total ban on hunting can we hope ever to save any of these magnificent creatures.

DISAPPEARING LIMBS

Thirty-seven million years ago, *Basilosaurus* – a primitive, 60-foot-long whale now long extinct and depicted here chasing its mate – cruised the Oligocene waters. It was during this time that toothed whales began to replace earlier, more primitive species. The hind limbs of earlier whales, meanwhile, are thought to have become so reduced that by the time *Basilosaurus* had evolved, they were hardly visible or nonexistent. Its fossils were first discovered in Egypt, but it probably swam in all the world's warmer oceans.

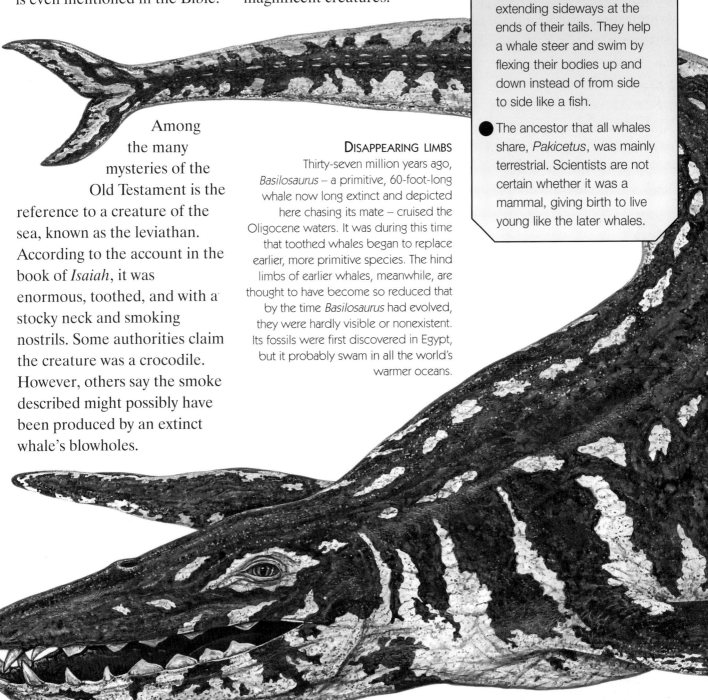

Fact file

● The ancient Tethys (TETH-IS) Sea, which 45 million years ago existed where western India is today, was once populated by several small species of early whales. Scientists think that some of them looked more like walruses than the whales we know today.

● Even the earliest true whales probably had flukes extending sideways at the ends of their tails. They help a whale steer and swim by flexing their bodies up and down instead of from side to side like a fish.

● The ancestor that all whales share, *Pakicetus*, was mainly terrestrial. Scientists are not certain whether it was a mammal, giving birth to live young like the later whales.

LIVING FOSSILS

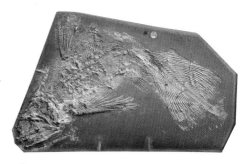

Remains of coelacanths (SEEL-A-KANTHS) have been found in rocks almost 400 million years old. That means they existed long before dinosaurs first evolved. Then in 1938 came a big surprise – the chance discovery of a live specimen!

SET IN STONE
This fine Jurassic coelacanth fossil comes from the collection at the Natural History Museum, London, England.

It was the naturalist Marjorie Courtenay-Latimer who took the initial step toward identification of a present-day coelacanth caught in 1938 and now on display in the East London Museum in South Africa. At the time she was a curator there and sought the opinion of a certain Professor J.L.B. Smith, then a leading expert on prehistoric marine life, who convinced her that what had been hauled ashore by fishermen in their nets was indeed a coelacanth. Its soft parts, however, had been thrown away, and only the skeleton remained.

Smith now determined to find another live specimen, offering a reward for any such discovery; and amazingly, one did turn up.

It was in the possession of a fisherman living in the Comoro Islands in the Indian Ocean, who had thoughtfully preserved it so that its flesh would not decay. With the help of an army aircraft loaned by the government of South Africa, Professor Smith rushed to see it, and before long the find made headline news right around the globe.

The coelacanth was clearly an odd creature; and Professor Smith even went so far as to suggest that it might have been able to walk upright on the seabed, using its flippers.

Later, marine biologist Hans Fricke from Germany's Max Planck Institute for Animal Behavior went in search of further live coelacanths and was equally fortunate.

With the help of local fishermen, who told how this fish's outer coating had once been used by them as a substitute for sandpaper, the team managed to locate several of these throwbacks to ancient times in their natural habitat.

FISHY MYSTERY
It is still a source of wonder to paleontologists and the public alike that the coelacanth managed to survive undetected for so many millions of years. What other surprises may the oceans still have in store?

Fricke saw them swimming in many ways, including backward and even upside down, and he has suggested that the curious handstands they sometimes do may be evidence of an ability to recognize each other and their prey through electrical fields.

How, then, have coelacanths managed to survive as a species for so long?

According to one theory, it may be because they inhabit deep waters, particularly during the day. Here, there are probably few rival species and so no great competition for the little food there is at such depths. They may also have swum up to feed at night while much other marine life rested.

So far live coelacanths have only been discovered in the Indian Ocean off Africa. Yet, strangely, a 17th-century Spanish image of one has been found.

BORN SURVIVOR
Described as possibly the greatest zoological event of the 20th century, the discovery of live coelacanths has proved an inspiration to paleontologists and naturalists alike throughout the world.

Fact file

- The species of coelacanth found by Marjorie Courtenay-Latimer was given the scientific name *Latimeria chalumnae* (LAT-IM-AIR-EE-AH CHAL-UM-NEYE.)

- Previously, coelacanths were thought to have died out 65 million years ago.

- After the initial discovery a further specimen was found by a fisherman off a small island in an archipelago northwest of Madagascar, which lies off eastern Africa in the Indian Ocean.

- The first coelacanths to be found were males. But in 1954 a female came to light.

- Most of those found have been taken from deep waters.

It is in the form of a silver statuette from a church in Bilbao, northern Spain. The delicately carved features make the fish instantly identifiable as a coelacanth. Yet we know this creature was only rediscovered elsewhere as a live species in 1938. Scientists therefore question whether coelacanths might still be alive in other seas, whether the portrait was made by a traveler to southern Africa, or whether it was based on fossilized remains.

SEA COWS

Huge, intelligent, and extremely slow-moving, Steller's sea cows are known to have been highly considerate to one another, even sometimes risking their own lives in the brotherly attempt to save a member of their own species seen to be in danger for its life.

When Vitus Bering's ship, the *St. Peter*, was wrecked in 1741 on an island later given his name, among those who survived was Georg Wilhelm Steller, a naturalist who was also acting as ship's doctor. Here in the shallow waters around the island he came across a fascinating sea cow.

ALL AT SEA
The photograph *left* shows a manatee, a type of sea cow, currently severely endangered in both Mediterranean and Caribbean waters.

By all accounts it was an enormous creature and one whose flesh would have provided numerous meals for the remaining crew. This was just as well since there was little else to be found on Bering Island to sustain the men.

Up to 30 feet in length and weighing around 6 tons, it lived mostly on a diet of seaweed and is thought to have been related to the elephant. Forty men were needed to haul one ashore after it had been harpooned. When cooked, the meat of this sea cow was said to be more delicious than beef.

Twenty-seven years after its discovery by Steller, however, the creature was extinct.

A SIMILAR FATE?

The dugong, *above*, also called a sea cow because it grazes on sea grass, is still harpooned for its flesh and currently endangered. It is now only found around Australia and the Red Sea.

Hundreds of them, living in herds, had been hunted for food, and this sea cow population thus became totally depleted. Indeed, Georg Steller seems to have been the last to see the creature named after him. But other types of sea cow have since also become imperiled for similar reasons.

CAUGHT UP IN IT

The dugong, for example, is constantly sought after not only for its meat but also its hide and its oil, which is valued in some parts of the world as an aphrodisiac and a medicine for treating headaches and constipation. But a dugong's death may also occur through the negligence of fishermen if, possibly along with its calves, it becomes trapped in a huge expanse of fishing nets.

COLLISION COURSE

Similar in appearance to Steller's sea cow and the dugong, the manatee is also vulnerable to being hunted by humans. But many deaths have been due to collisions with watercraft, possibly because of the manatee's shortsightedness. An organization known as the Save the Manatee Club is, however, doing its best to raise money to support conservation of this mammal in the Caribbean.

Fact file

- According to Steller, instead of teeth, these plant-eating sea cows had horny plates set in their gums. The plates were used for cutting and grinding up their intake of vegetation.

- The ends of the front limbs of a Steller's sea cow (there were no back limbs) were like hooves but more pointed, and would have been useful for tearing up seaweed.

- Steller observed that gulls would often settle on the backs of these sea cows to feast on the bugs that had infested their skin.

- The scientific name for Steller's sea cow is *Hydrodamalis gigas* (HEYE-DROH-DAM-AH-LIS GIG-AS). An adult measured about 30 feet in length.

HARPOON HORROR

The illustration *below* shows a Steller's sea cow being harpooned. These mighty creatures would be dragged ashore so the carcasses could be cut up and cooked for a filling and tasty meal.

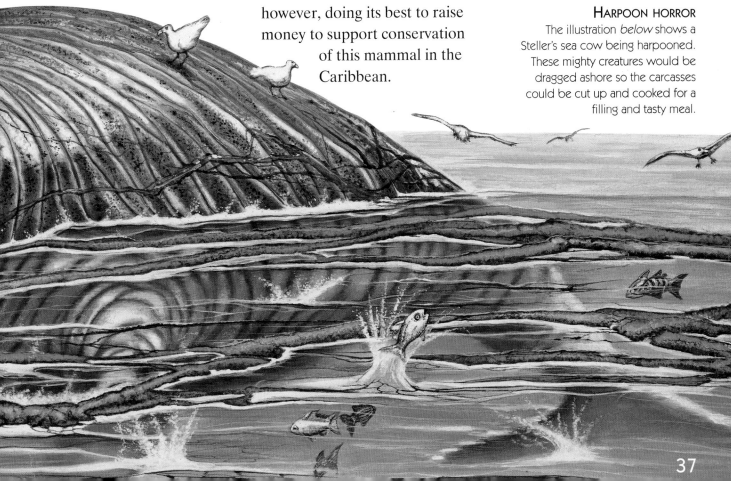

WEST INDIAN MONK SEAL

Back in the 15th century the famous explorer Christopher Columbus sighted several of these seals, which have not been seen since 1952, in the Caribbean Ocean. Unfortunately, he started a trend that eventually led to their demise.

Seal flesh is certainly not widely eaten today. But in some parts of the world, at various times, these creatures were killed in large numbers, mostly for their blubber, from which oil could also be extracted, perhaps for lamps prior to use of electricity.

We even know from contemporary accounts that Columbus gave specific instructions to his crew to kill eight Caribbean monk seals when other food supplies had run out.

CRY FREEDOM
It is not hard to imagine the desperate barking of the millions of Caribbean monk seals as, over the centuries, one by one, they fell victim to greedy hunters.

After this sea wolves, as the monk seals were also known, were increasingly hunted commercially, as well as by local fishermen for their own consumption. There are even accounts of shipwrecked travelers who survived by feeding on them. Small wonder, then, that over the centuries these gentle giants of the sea began to die out as a species. Indeed, an aerial survey carried out in the Caribbean in 1973 produced no evidence at all of their survival in these waters.

Between six and nine feet in length, and weighing as much as 500 pounds when fully grown, the Caribbean monk seal is thought to have existed for millions of years before it finally disappeared. What remains a mystery, however, is how this tropical seal, a relative of those from Antarctica, reached its warm Caribbean habitat.

ON VOYAGES OF DISCOVERY
Columbus, *left*, and his crew killed a number of monk seals off a Caribbean island near what is now Haiti, as did the 16th-century explorer Ponce de León, who reached Florida and Puerto Rico.

Several other adventurers and historians have also written about the taking of monk seals. One shipwrecked 16th-century Spanish diarist, for instance, recorded that at the Florida Keys, where they were also to be found:

"*Some feast on sea wolves; but not all of them because there is a distinction between the upper and the lower classes, but the most important people dine on them.*"

More recently, another traveler to these parts wrote that: "*The Bahamas are filled with seals. Sometimes fishers will catch one hundred in a night.*"

Once culls had reached that sort of level at the turn of the 20th century, it would have been impossible to maintain the population. The Caribbean monk seal only bred once a year; and because it was not aggressive by nature, it also proved to be an easy victim for sharks sharing these waters.

A log held by Great Britain's Public Record Office provides evidence, too, that in 1742 many of these seals were killed by the starving crew of a warship marooned in the Carribean. Spanish navigators who sailed to this part of the world, meanwhile, would use the monk seals' fat to paint the bottom of their ships in an attempt to prevent leakage. Some are also known to have been killed by scientists for display as museum specimens, until the species was officially declared extinct in 1996.

SEALED FATE?

Others met a cruel and unnecessary end when they were shot about 100 years ago and their skins put to use by a then flourishing fur trade that manufactured purses and coats from their pelts.

What, though, of others of this family that inhabit the world's warm waters?

Fact file

● The scientific name for the extinct Caribbean monk seal is *Monachus tropicalis* (MOHN-AH-KUS TROP-EE-KAHL-IS). The surviving Hawaiian species is known by naturalists as *Monachus schauinlandis* (SHAU-IN-LAND-IS), while two repeated words, *Monachus monachus*, are used by experts to refer to the Mediterranean variety.

● A Caribbean monk seal was seen at Key West, Florida, in 1922, but was shot. The last confirmed sighting of this seal was made 30 years later, at a place called Serranilla Bank in the Caribbean Ocean.

● Caribbean monk seals were once given the popular name of sea wolves (or *lobos marinos*) by the Spanish who came to this region.

WATER BABIES
Graceful swimmers and very tame, Caribbean monk seals like the one *above* came ashore to give birth to live young, who soon took readily to the water.

Sadly, the Hawaiian and Mediterranean species of monk seals are severely endangered today, but every effort is being made to help them survive.

Even the sharks of prehistoric times did not reach anywhere near the size of mighty *Dunkleosteus* (<u>DUNK</u>-LEE-<u>OST</u>-EE-US), *below*, a sea creature which grew to be 40 feet in length, and which was characterized by an enormous head at least eight times the size of yours.

Dunkleosteus, also known as *Dinichthys* (DIN-<u>IKT</u>-IS), was probably the ultimate ruler of the Devonian seas and a highly formidable predator. As a typical placoderm, it had a plated head, and the back of its body, though flexible, was covered with thick scales.

But the most distinctive features of this marine marvel were its enormous jaws, which were lined not with teeth but a series of bony, triangular projections. Each was as sharp as a razorblade, and a single bite would have resulted in several terrible wounds.

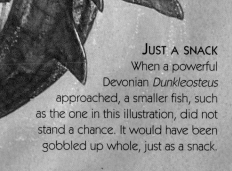

JUST A SNACK
When a powerful Devonian *Dunkleosteus* approached, a smaller fish, such as the one in this illustration, did not stand a chance. It would have been gobbled up whole, just as a snack.

By Carboniferous times, however – that is, 360-290 million years ago – placoderms had all but disappeared, and their place was taken by various types of sharks, also famous for their fearsome jaws.

Some are in fact only known from their teeth, and thereby hangs a curious tale. During the 17th century items known as "tongue-stones" were sold to tourists as lucky charms on Malta until a Danish zoologist, Niels Steensen, when traveling to this Mediterranean island, recognized them for what they really were – the fossilized teeth of long extinct sharks.

A number, like *Pleuracanthus* (<u>PLOOR</u>-AK-<u>AN</u>-THUS), lived in the freshwater environment of Carboniferous lakes and rivers, but they were small in comparison with today's sharks and grew to just over 2 feet long. But in spite of that they were predatory and caught smaller fish in their gaping jaws.

This particular shark also bore a long spine behind its head. Scientists are not sure about the function of this appendage, but it may have been a weapon or perhaps helped the shark find its direction in some way.

Paleontologists digging in Ohio found fairly complete remains of another early shark, *Cladoselache* (<u>KLAD</u>-OSS-<u>EE</u>-LAK). Remarkably, it had large eyes; and so, unlike modern sharks, probably hunted during the day and by sight, not mainly by a sense of smell.

LONG IN THE TOOTH
The small tooth, *above right*, is from a modern great white shark. It is tiny in comparison with the one on the *left*, which comes from a giant extinct species.

It is generally assumed some species of early sharks perished in the mass extinction that occurred at the end of Permian times, 250 million years ago. (You can read about this in the volume *Why Extinction Occurs*.) But a few survived, though numbers would have been drastically depleted.

Sharks more like those we know today then arose in Triassic times and continued to evolve into creatures with wider-opening mouths, longer upper jaws, and bulletlike bodies. Some are known as mixed-tooth sharks, with flattened back teeth ideal for crunching on mollusks. But at the end of Jurassic times sharks divided into two main groups. One gave rise to species of shark like those of the modern era; others evolved into skates and rays.

OPEN WIDE!
This photograph of a child standing in the fossilized jaws of a shark gives an indication of the tremendous size of some of these extinct species.

Fact file

- Sharks first began to evolve about 360 million years ago.

- Early sharks, now extinct, looked very different from those we know today. Some , for instance, had a bony spine rising above their heads. It may have been used to ward off rivals in territorial disputes or by males when fighting over a mate.

- All known extinct sharks had streamlined bodies, just like those of today, which helped them swim at great speed.

- Most sharks today are predatory, and many will devour humans given the opportunity. Some, however, have evolved to feed on plankton. They include the 45-foot long basking shark and the even longer whale shark.

VANISHING REEFS

Poor or unclean water spells the death knell for a coral reef. Sunlight must be allowed to penetrate so that the algae on which it is dependent can thrive. But this ideal environment is fast disappearing in some parts of the world. So might coral one day become extinct?

CONSERVE OUR CORAL!
Once as vibrant as traditional Persian carpets, some of the world's highly sensitive reefs have been suffocated to death by pollutants, while others have been killed off in one fell swoop through use of explosives for mining in the sea.

A coral reef may look just like a huge expanse of inanimate, colorful rock; but on the surface there is a thriving mass of small, live, fleshy organisms, collectively known as polyps, and plant life, too.

Found only in fairly shallow tropical waters and in a bewildering variety of shapes – everything from fanlike forms to branches that resemble a deer's antlers – coral is part of the world's oldest ecosystem. It grows continually and is self-repairing. Indeed, the 19th-century scientist Charles Darwin, father of the theory of evolution, was the first to realize changes occur as new reefs form on the framework of older, dead structures.

But even the magnificent Great Barrier Reef, which lies off the east coast of Australia and is the largest organic structure of any kind in the world, is not immune to frequent exploitation of its resources. In fact, there are many threats to the delicate ecological balance of all the world's reefs.

REEFS AT RISK
The environment of a reef, like the one shown here, is finely balanced and often at risk from divers, coral collectors, pollution, and companies exploring for oil and minerals.

DOING DAMAGE

Coral reefs are formed from limestone, which industry widely puts to a whole range of practical uses. Taking limestone in this way causes terrible destruction to a reef and may also affect a neighboring coastline, which will only too readily become eroded.

In many respects coral reefs are like the rain forests of the seas, and both have become endangered through human intervention. But weather can sometimes destroy them, too. Hurricanes, for example, have been known to reduce some Caribbean reefs to nothing but rubble; although if subsequent circumstances are favorable, they will grow back within a few decades. Reefs off Colombia and Ecuador, both in South America, have been severely affected by adverse weather conditions, too.

Pollution is another major damaging factor. About 30% of the reef off Florida's Key Largo has already been damaged, for instance. Oil spills have also killed off large parts of some of the world's reefs.

THE NEED TO ACT NOW

Reefs have existed for countless millions of years. But at the time of each prehistoric mass extinction paleontologists can tell that they disappeared along with all sorts of other marine and land life. They also say it could easily happen again.

Scientists have estimated that if the tropical seas warm up by as little as one or two degrees during this century, the sensitive environment of a reef may become so seriously damaged that it could die off altogether.

In fact, global warming is a very real threat to all reefs and of course in turn to the wide variety of life they sustain. But extreme cold can kill reefs too. So it seems that only climate control, together with the complete nonintervention of humans, could ever provide the world's coral reefs with some sort of guarantee for an entirely secure future.

HOT NEWS

Excessively high sea temperatures are another factor that may sometimes be to blame for damaged coral. In the photograph of part of a reef off New South Wales, Australia, *right*, you can see that some has been bleached from its original strong brown coloring to a soft shade of pink.

Fact file

- Coral is formed from the outer skeletons of animals known as polyps. Most are only about the size of one of the letters in this printed sentence.

- There are three main types of coral reefs. Fringing reefs occur in shallow waters along a coastline. Barrier reefs are separated from the shore by shallow lakes or lagoons; and atolls are small island reefs surrounded by deep lagoons.

- Australia's Great Barrier Reef, which scientists think first started to evolve around 18 million years ago, covers an enormous area – 80,000 square miles in all.

- Many countries with waters where coral reefs are to be found are working actively to prevent pollution of their seas.

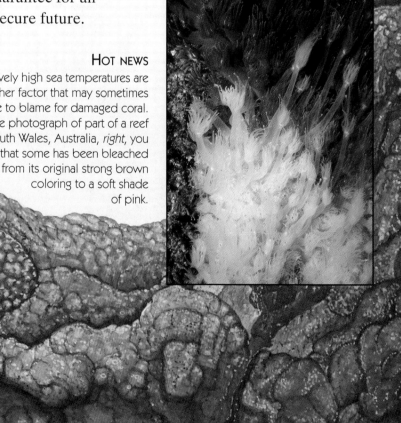

TOMORROW'S SEAS

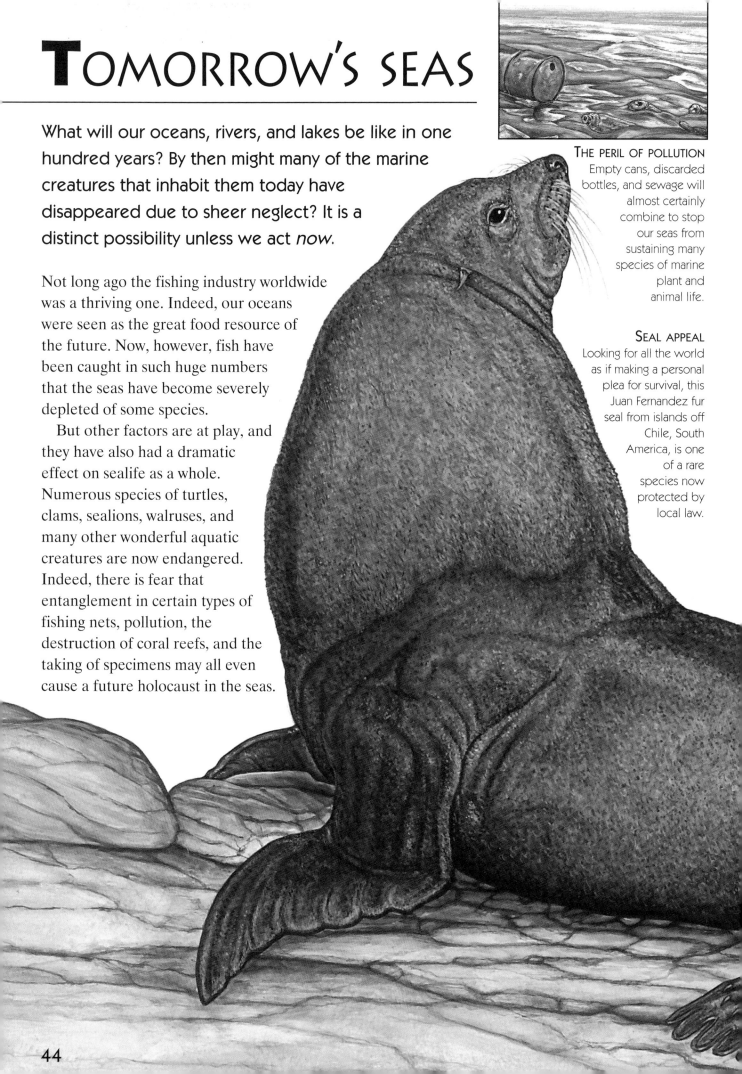

What will our oceans, rivers, and lakes be like in one hundred years? By then might many of the marine creatures that inhabit them today have disappeared due to sheer neglect? It is a distinct possibility unless we act *now*.

Not long ago the fishing industry worldwide was a thriving one. Indeed, our oceans were seen as the great food resource of the future. Now, however, fish have been caught in such huge numbers that the seas have become severely depleted of some species.

But other factors are at play, and they have also had a dramatic effect on sealife as a whole. Numerous species of turtles, clams, sealions, walruses, and many other wonderful aquatic creatures are now endangered. Indeed, there is fear that entanglement in certain types of fishing nets, pollution, the destruction of coral reefs, and the taking of specimens may all even cause a future holocaust in the seas.

THE PERIL OF POLLUTION
Empty cans, discarded bottles, and sewage will almost certainly combine to stop our seas from sustaining many species of marine plant and animal life.

SEAL APPEAL
Looking for all the world as if making a personal plea for survival, this Juan Fernandez fur seal from islands off Chile, South America, is one of a rare species now protected by local law.

REPLENISHING THE SEA

What, then, can be done to prevent further disaster? First and foremost, every effort must speedily be made to restore stocks of fish, which will also go some way to providing for larger marine species affected by a shortage of food.

With the humpback, fin, right, and blue species of whales all now severely endangered, many of the world's countries have finally agreed to put firm restrictions on whaling. Through legislation, industry can also be prevented from polluting our waters, and that not only means the sea but rivers and lakes, too.

Education about the effects of introducing new species will also be helpful. In 1958, for instance, the Nile perch was introduced into part of Lake Victoria, East Africa, as a potentially rich food source. But before long this fish took over the lake completely.

WASTE NOT!

Many countries of the world have already wisely taken strong action by introducing legislation to prevent industry pouring harmful chemicals and other noxious waste into the oceans.

Established fish declined, and local African fishermen lost their livelihood, too, because the population of this region did not seem to like perch very much anyway. To make matters worse, this is exactly the sort of situation that cannot easily be reversed.

But while humans have been been maltreating underwater life, the Pacific has harbored a secret only revealed by scientists in 1977. Here, at over 8,000 feet below the surface, in this desolate environment they found colonies of tiny creatures never seen before.

STACKS OF FOOD

Vents like chimney stacks, found deep in the Pacific Ocean, emit sulfur poisonous to most creatures but not to the bacteria that thrive on it, and that are then eaten by recently discovered vent animals.

Fact file

● In some parts of the world dangerous radioactive waste has been dumped in our seas. It is sealed in concrete but there is concern that before it breaks down and becomes safe, which can take thousands of years, it might accidentally leak and cause havoc in the oceans.

● The dumping of untreated sewage is a threat to sealife, too. Human waste can provide lots of nutrients for underwater plants. But there is risk of overfeeding, so that too much oxygen is used up, and little remains to sustain underwater animal life.

● If pollutants such as mercury and DDT are allowed to enter the food chain through contaminated fish, the results can be devastating.

Their habitat is hot, mineral-rich water gushing from vents that rise from the ocean floor. The seas, if not neglected today, may yield wondrous surprises tomorrow.

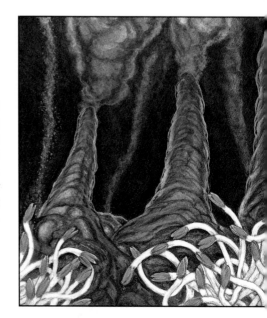

GLOSSARY

ammonite
an extinct soft-bodied aquatic creature with a coiled shell

archelon
a large prehistoric turtle

arthropods
a group of invertebrates with jointed bodies and limbs, including insects and spiders

beached
brought ashore from the ocean

belemnites
extinct, marine, squidlike fossils

calcite
a mineral

Carboniferous times
a period lasting from about 345 to 280 million years ago

coelacanth
a rediscovered ancient fish

continental shelf
a gently sloping zone under shallow seas near a coastline

coral
the skeletal remains of various small marine invertebrates

Cretaceous times
a period lasting from about 144 to 65 million years ago

cryptozoologist
a scientist looking for evidence of survival of long-lost creatures

detritus
substances that have worn away gradually from rock

Devonian times
a period lasting from about 395 to 345 million years ago

Eocene times
a period lasting from about 50 to 24 million years ago

fluke
the end of a whale's tail

fossil
animal or plant remains embedded or preserved in rocks or other material

hermaphrodite
a creature with both male and female organs

ichthyosaur
an extinct marine reptile with a fishlike body and a long snout

Jurassic times
a period lasting from about 213 to 144 million years ago

landlubber
dwelling on or preferring land

limestone
rock comprising mainly calcium carbonate

mesosaur
a prehistoric freshwater reptile with webbed feet and toothed jaws

mosasaur
a large, muscular, prehistoric marine reptile with sharp teeth

Oligocene times
a period lasting from about 22 to 15 million years ago

paleontologist
a scientist who studies fossils

Permian times
a period lasting from about 280 to 230 million years ago

placoderm
an early fish with a jawbone

placodont
a Triassic semiaquatic reptile

plankton
small marine organisms, usually found floating on water

plesiosaur
a long-necked marine reptile from prehistoric times

pliosaur
a large-jawed, thick-necked prehistoric marine reptile

thorax
part of an animal between the head and the abdomen

Triassic times
a period lasting from about 249 to 213 million years ago

trilobite
a small, extinct marine creature

vertebra
part of the backbone